Dear Coach,

A collection of texts, emails and unmentionables from the front lines of youth sports.

by,

Rizer Brown

A special thanks to all the parents out there who have completely lost their perspective. Without you, this book wouldn't be possible.

Inbox — Yahoo! (17756 messages)

oo! (4094) ⌄   Flagged   Drafts (4) ⌄

████

To: ████

Re: Emails etc

No. Couldn't deal with the parents :-)

> On May 10, 2017, at 2:38 PM, █████████████████████████ wrote:
>
> Yes. I will change the names, genders and sports, plus I will create fake email accounts, etc. Tha
> the U12 team?
>
> Rizer

> On May 10, 2017, at 2:34 PM, █████████████████████████ wrote:
>
> Hi Rizer,
>
> The emails are attached. You're gonna change the names right?
>
> J

Contents

Asshole soccer dad

Burned out Ted

Greg gone wild

Suck up lax mom

Texting parents

Hockey coach confidential

*Any texts, emails, and other scenarios that bare a striking similarity
to something you said or did is a coincidence. A very unfortunate coincidence.*

I've been thinking a lot about this and I think it would be a good idea for you to email the coach. We spend a lot of time and money on this team and ultimately we have a right to circle back to him and discuss our concerns. I would keep the email very light and reasonable. I don't think we need to go to any extremes at this point.

March 2, 2017 6:00 PM
Phil Webb Phil@BigBank.net
To: Jim Black jimandkaren@organics.org
Re: Problem player

Dear Coach,

Just wanted to share some thoughts with you on todays game. We definitely played hard and it was a disappointing loss. I was able to identify one weak link on the team that created most of the turnovers. Number three. He doesn't want the ball. At one point he sat down. Literally sat down. Would it be possible to bench him during the last five minutes of a close game? A couple of parents were talking about this and it seems like the right thing to do.

Looking forward to your thoughts,

Phil
(Lucas #7)

March 2, 2017 6:10 PM
Jim Black jimandkaren@organics.org
To: Phil Webb Phil@BigBank.net
Re: Problem Player

Hi Phil,

Thanks for attending todays game. This is a kindergarten rec team. We don't bench kids.

Thanks,

Jim
"Peace begins with a smile" - Mother Teresa

Ted Nichols TdN@hotmail.com
To: Girls Varsity Parents   March 15, 2017 at 10 AM
Re: Code of Conduct Reminder

Hi Trident Parents,

Welcome to another season of soccer! I am really looking forward to coaching your girls! As many of you know, I'm a big fan of setting expectations. In that vein, I want to remind everyone of our school policy related to sideline conduct. Please refrain from yelling at the following people:

> 1) the players and coaches of the opposing team
> 2) the referees
> 3) the parents of the opposing team
> 4) kids on our team who aren't playing the way you would like
> 5) me
> 6) your player
> 7) parents of players on our team.

Please refrain from the following behaviors:

> 1) running down the sideline when your player has the ball suggesting plays
> 2) calling out plays you feel would better suit the situation
> 3) coming over to the player bench to talk to your player mid-game
> 4) coming over to talk to me mid-game.
> 4) holding up signs with plays
> 5) kicking objects
> 6) throwing chairs
> 7) drinking alcohol

Here are some books and links that I have found helpful as both a parent and a coach:

No Stress Youth Sports by Chad Bumble
Playing and Winning Without Whining by Kevin Almost

www.fairyouthsportsassoc.com

Thanks so much. It's gonna be a great season! -Coach Ted

March 17, 2017 at 9:34 PM
Greg Smith greg@donots.com
To: Ben Rodgers rodgersconsulting12@gmail.com
Re: Confused

Hi Ben,
I enjoyed watching the boys play Belmont this morning.
Is there a reason why Caleb didn't get off the bench?
Greg Smith
(Caleb #9)

March 18, 2017 at 8:10 AM
Ben Rodgers rodgersconsulting12@gmail.com
To: Greg Smith greg@donots.com
Re: Confused

Hi Greg,
The Hawks is an elite team and all players are told at the start of the season that they earn their playing time during games by way of effort during practice.
Ben

March 18, 2017 at 8:11 AM
Greg Smith greg@donots.com
To: Ben Rodgers rodgersconsulting12@gmail.com
Re: Confused
Are you saying he's not playing well during practice? -Greg

March 18, 2017 at 8:20 AM
Ben Rodgers rodgersconsulting12@gmail.com
To: Greg Smith greg@donots.com
Re: Confused

That's correct.
Ben

March 18, 2017 at 8:32 AM
Greg Smith greg@donots.com
To: Ben Rodgers rodgersconsulting12@gmail.com
Re: Confused

Both my wife and I are very driven athletes. I attend a boot camp every morning before work, and most days, I'm not even tired afterwards.That's the mind set of our house; all-in 24/7. Confidentially, Caleb is complicated because he's a genius (IQ of 142) and he over thinks things. He is basically a machine that no one has figured out how to start yet. A machine that could be galvanized into a force of nature. Give him some playing time and you will see what you're dealing with. He is a triple threat; drive, brains, speed.

Greg

March 18, 2017 at 8:50 AM
Ben Rodgers rodgersconsulting12@gmail.com
To: Greg Smith greg@donots.com
Re: Confused

I'd like to see Caleb stop chewing gum with his mouth guard in. I think that'd be a good place to start.

Ben

Ted Nichols TdN@hotmail.com
To: Girls Varsity Parents
Re: Code of conduct questions

April 17, 2017 at 7:34 AM

Hi Trident parents,

I've had a few questions regarding what types of things we would prefer you not yell at the kids. As always, encouragement is great. Generally we'd prefer you refrain from yelling anything negative. Also, please don't coach the kids. That's my job. Just enjoy the game.

We still need a parent volunteer to bring orange slices.

Thanks.

Really looking forward to this season. Great group of girls!

Coach Ted

Ted Nichols TdN@hotmail.com
To: Girls Varsity Parents   April 17, 2017 at 8:56 PM
Re: Follow up on conduct

Hi Trident Parents,

After today's game it appears I need to be more specific. Please do not yell any of the following:

"Pass the ball!"
"Shoot it!"
"Are you serious?"
"Are you fucking serious."
"Are you blind?"
"Wake up!"
"Really? Really?"
"Ref you suck."

Some additional books that you may find helpful:

How To Support Your Young Athlete by Mindy Lincoln PhD & Julie Benzo LICSW, MPH

Driven too far by Matt Lewis

Thanks. It's going to be a great season.

Coach Ted

May 5, 2017 at 5:13 PM
Molly Green laxmommie@gmail.com
To: Team Moms bbc: Hank Rawlings hr200@us.gov
Re: Surprise Coach gift 💔

Hi Moms,
I'm organizing a gift for coach Rawlings. People can contribute whatever they like. Twenty dollars a family would be great if you can swing it. Dan and I may do a little more than that because we feel he deserves something really special. Please have your boys give me your cash / check at practice. Whatever you can do is fine.

Molly
(Evan #13)

May 5, 2017 at 5:26 PM
Hank Rawlings hr200@us.gov
To: Molly Green laxmommie@gmail.com
Re: Surprise Coach gift 💔

Hi Molly,

Was I supposed to be bcc'd on this email? - Hank

May 5, 2017 at 5:28 PM
Molly Green laxmommie@gmail.com
To: Hank Rawlings hr200@us.gov
Re: Surprise Coach gift 💔

Oops. Total mistake 😬. - Molly

May 5, 2017 at 5:30 PM
Hank Rawlings hr200@us.gov
To: Molly Green laxmommie@gmail.com
Re: Surprise Coach gift 💔

No worries. Thanks for thinking of me. —H

May 5, 2017 at 5:31 PM
Molly Green laxmommie@gmail.com
To: Hank Rawlings hr200@us.gov
Re: Surprise Coach gift 💝

Absolutely! You deserve it!!! 👍😍BTW. When are tryouts for next season?

May 5, 2017 at 9:37 PM
Hank Rawlings hr200@us.gov
To: Molly Green laxmommie@gmail.com
Re: Surprise Coach gift 💝

Mid August. Have a great Sunday! -H

May 5, 2017 at 9:41 PM
Molly Green laxmommie@gmail.com
To: Hank Rawlings   hr200@us.gov
Re: Surprise Coach gift 💝

How do you think Evan looks?

May 5, 2017 at 10:57 PM
Hank Rawlings hr200@us.gov
To: Molly Green laxmommie@gmail.com
Re: Surprise Coach gift 💝
The kids will all show up at tryouts and do their best.

May 5, 2017 at 11:01 PM
Molly Green laxmommie@gmail.com
To: Hank Rawlings hr200@us.gov
Re: Surprise Coach gift 💝
Now I'm worried.😱 Are you cutting Evan?

Today, 7:33 PM

How's practice

you're not gonna believe who mad the team

The point guard 🐌

yup back on the team

Wtf

she just set a screen for no one

What's Lila doing

looks not great. not sure whats up with her

I'd like to see more hustle.

just missed a basket

Delivered

March 16, 2017 3:10 AM
Greg Smith greg@donots.com
To: Ben Rodgers <u>rodgersconsulting12@gmail.com</u>
Re: Cool pic of Caleb

Hi Coach, I stumbled across this picture of Caleb at 8 months and I thought you might enjoy it. Around this age was when we noticed he was ambidextrous. Absolutely no problem transitioning a toy from one hand to the other, and back.

In this photo he has just had the toy in his left hand when he suddenly (and I remember this because it was like a rocket) threw the toy to his right hand.
I remember this moment so clearly. My wife grabbed the camera and we watched him for about an hour basically own this toy. To put it bluntly, this toy was his bitch. At that point we knew we had something really special on our hands. Caleb often exhibits this kind of freak athletic ability during moments when no one is looking. I wonder if perhaps that is what is happening at practice? You're just missing it because he is so quick? I have addressed the gum chewing. Sorry about that!

Greg

May 20, 2017 at 5:18 PM
Phil **Webb** Phil@BigBank.net
To: Jim Black jimandkaren@organics.org
Re: Problem Player

Dear Coach,

Another tough loss. Same issue; number three. I took the liberty of pulling that kid aside after the game yesterday. After he caught the ball with his hands I wondered if perhaps he thought he was playing basketball instead of soccer. Turns out, he has no idea what he's doing, and frankly he's not that committed. I didn't get a response, zero. Kid just stared at me. I think that kid has to go. And where are his parents?

May 20, 2017 at 8:31 PM
Jim Black jimandkaren@organics.org
To: Phil Webb Phil@BigBank.net
Re: Problem Player

Phill,

I believe you are talking about Jose. He doesn't speak English. His family just moved here from Columbia. His father plays for the Seattle Sounders and he was traveling with his team. Jose's mother is at all the games but she just watches, no shouting. Most of this is probably none of your business.

Jim
"Peace begins with a smile" - Mother Teresa

Ted Nichols TdN@hotmail.com   May 22, 2017 at 9:34 PM
To: Girls Varsity Parents
Re: Incredibly disappointed

Trident parents,

I have received several inquires about the fight in the parking lot after Saturday's game with SouthWest. While I can't get into specific details, I can tell you that both people involved were arrested and as a consequence, they are banned from school grounds indefinitely. As a result of this incident we will be holding an emergency parent meeting right after practice Monday. Also, does anyone know anything about who created the Facebook page "SouthWest Parents Suck." Please email me directly.

I have added the following rules to our conduct guidelines. Engaging in these behaviors will result in your child's immediate removal from the team:

> 8) Planning altercations with other parents on school grounds.
> 9) Creating negative social media pages about other programs.
> 10) Leaving feces on the hood of an opposing team parent's car.

I am going to ask that every parent read this book; My Parents Ruined My Love of the Game by Buck Bentley and go to this website; www.theproblemwithyouthsports.org

Coach

Margaret Adams marg_a@aol.com   May 22, 2017 at 10:12 PM
To: Ted Nichols TdN@hotmail.com
Re: Incredibly disappointed

Hi Coach,
I'm pretty sure David Hillman left the cup of "stuff" on someone's car. He didn't want to leave the game and just went in a cup. It was such a nail bitter, no one wanted to miss anything.
We all smelled it. -Margy

May 24, 2017 8:12 PM
Ben Rodgers rodgersconsulting12@gmail.com
To: 5/6 Elite Hawk Boys Parents
bbc: Boys 5/6 Elite Coaches
Re: Note on my windshield

Hi Parents,

This note was on my windshield after the game last night. The best way to reach me is via email or my cell. Thanks. Ben

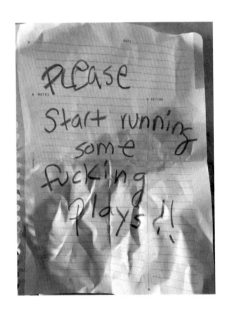

Ted Nichols TdN@hotmail.com
To: David Hillman DH_12@yahoo.com   May 25, 2017 at 8:19 PM
Re: South West Game Follow-up

Hi David,

I regret having to send you this email. As I'm sure you are aware, we had a very unfortunate incident after the South West game involving two parents. It later came to my attention that one of the South West parents found a cup of feces on the hood of their car. Another parent has come forward and reported that you were observed using a cup to relieve yourself during the game. As awkward as this email is, I need to let you know that the school takes this type of incident very seriously. Moving forward I would ask that if you were in fact involved, or needing to use the restroom, that this type of behavior never occur again. If I am incorrect, I apologize and please disregard this email.

Ted

David Hillman DH_12@yahoo.com
To: Ted Nichols TdN@hotmail.com   May 25, 2017 at 9:12 PM
Re: South West Game Follow-up

Ted.

I take full responsibility for my actions. It is not the first time I have had to take care of business during a close game. I am fairly adept at this technique and typically, unless I've had a huge lunch, no one notices. I agree that leaving feces on a car hood is problematic. I would never do that, nor did I do that Saturday. Typically I use a to-go cup that comes with a lid. I then discard the cup according to the trash choice directives. If available, the "compost" receptacle as that is usually the best choice. I am really angry that a parent from our team would represent our community so poorly and do something so disgusting as to leave a cup of waste on someones car. Between us, I find the sideline conduct of this group of parents really disturbing. Margaret Adams for instance has a nickname for every child on the team. She refers to my daughter as "Little Ms. Out-to-lunch." I have addressed this with her twice and she appears not to care. Just a heads up. -David

June 12, 2017 at 4:45 PM
Jim Black jimandkaren@organics.org
To: Phil Webb Phil@BigBank.net
Re: shirts / Sharpie???

Phil.

Jose's father called me and told me that a parent fitting your description gave Jose a Sharpie and a bag of Sounders t-shirts after practice today. Mr. Hernandez believes this was a request for his autograph and for him to sign the shirts. Mr. Hernandez would prefer this not occur again.

Jim
"Peace begins with a smile" - Mother Teresa

June 12, 2017 at 5:16 PM
Phil Webb Phil@BigBank.net
To: Jim Black jimandkaren@organics.org
Re: shirts / Sharpie???

Guilty. He's one of my favorite Sounders players. I'd actually love to grab a beer with him sometime. Can you forward me his contact info? Phil

June 12, 2017 at 5:21 PM
Phill Webb Phill@BigBank.net
To: Jim Black jimandkaren@organics.org
Re: shirts / Sharpie???

My son would also like to invite Jose over for a playdate. If you know where they live and could shoot me the address I could swing by and pick up Jose.

June 12, 2017 at 10:37 PM
Phill Webb Phill@BigBank.net
To: Jim Black jimandkaren@organics.org
Re: shirts / Sharpie???

You're probably jammed. No worries! I speak a little conversational Spanish. I'll talk to his mom at practice.

June 13, 2017 at 9:10
Ben Rodgers <u>rodgersconsulting12@gmail.com</u>
To: Boys 5/6 Elite Coaches
Re: Note

Check it out. Another note on my windshield.

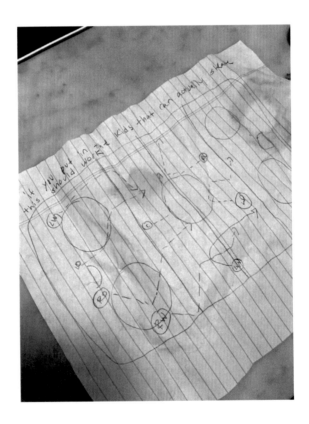

June 13, 2017 at 10:05 PM
David Brown brownfamily_1975@earthlink.net
To: Ben Rodgers rodgersconsulting12@gmail.com **Tom McDonald** tom_kath6@gmail.com **Jeff Sullivan**
SullyMA@aol.com;
Re: Re: Note

That play would never work with our kids. -DB

June 13, 2017 at 10:12 PM
Ben Rodgers rodgersconsulting12@gmail.com
To: **David Brown** brownfamily_1975@earthlink.net;**Tom McDonald** tom_kath6@gmail.com **Jeff Sullivan**
SullyMA@aol.com;
Re: Re: Note

No kidding.

June 13, 2017 at 10:15 PM
Tom McDonald tom_kath6@gmail.com
To: Ben Rodgers rodgersconsulting12@gmail.com **David Brown; Jeff Sullivan** SullyMA@aol.com;
David Brown brownfamily_1975@earthlink.net
Re: Re: Note

Who wants to wager on which parent is doing this? I vote Henry's dad.
Tom

June 13, 2017 at 10:34 PM
Jeff Sullivan SullyMA@aol.com
To: Ben Rodgers rodgersconsulting12@gmail.com **David Brown; Jeff Sullivan** SullyMA@aol.com;
David Brown brownfamily_1975@earthlink.net
Re: Re: Note

I've got 30 on Mikey's mom.

June 13, 2017 at 11:12 PM
Ben Rodgers rodgersconsutling12@gmail.com
To: **David Brown** brownfamily_1975@earthlink.net;**Tom McDonald** tom_kath6@gmail.com **Jeff Sullivan**
SullyMA@aol.com;

Super tough call. What if it's more then one?

June 13, 2017 at 11:38 PM
Jeff Sullivan SullyMA@aol.com
To: Ben Rodgers rodgersconsulting12@gmail.com **David Brown; Jeff Sullivan** SullyMA@aol.com;
David Brown brownfamily_1975@earthlink.net
Re: Re: Note

run

June 15, 2017 at 9:12 PM
Greg Smith greg@donots.com
To: Ben Rodgers <u>rodgersconsulting12@gmail.com</u>
Re: Caleb insights..

Hi There Coach!

Just wanted to follow up with an explanation on Caleb's gum chewing at practice. I found this picture of Caleb asleep with his pacifier. We think he probably has an oral fixation that is our fault. So the gum is on us. Let me expand. He was so bright as a baby he always needed something to do. I mean the kid was using a can opener at age five months. So at the advice of our pediatrician we gave Caleb a pacifier to occupy him and keep him away from the refried beans. To give you a sense of how smart he is, here's a quote from his psychological exam (it was recommended we have him tested in kindergarten because he was demonstrating some behaviors that suggested he needed to be more academically challenged. It wasn't because there was anything wrong with him, more like too much was right). Here's the quote: "Shows excessive focus on objects. Intense attention to detail."

I don't know about you, but I'm pretty sure attention to detail can't hurt when you're aiming for the net! I am happy to send his entire evaluation along if you're interested. That's his older brother to the left / your right. He plays Center for the Waltham High Rockets. He was a little before your time with the program. Unreal player. Full on weapon of mass destruction. He's less reserved then his brother, more of a hands on guy. Anyway, really hoping Caleb will get off the bench this weekend!

June 15, 2017 at 9:30 PM
Ben Rodgers rodgersconsulting12@gmail.com
To: Greg Smithgreg@donots.com
Re: Caleb Insights..

Hi Greg,

thanks for the information. i'm going to pass on reading his evaluation. see you at the game

June 15, 2017 at 2:12 AM
Greg Smith greg@donots.com
To: Ben Rodgers rodgersconsulting12@gmail.com
Re: Genetics

Wow! Just stumbled across a great pix of my dad's D1 Hockey team. Can't remember if I mentioned my father was an All-American. He's top left, and was left dominant, but could really go right or left. Also loves gum. Go figure :-)

Today 4:53 PM

that dad you can't stand just came over here and asked if lila was trying out for the travel team🙄

Lets not tip our hand. his daughter is decent

element of surprise??

I think he can sweat it out till tryouts

Maybe we should say we aren't trying out and then show up? BAM! That should rattle them

BAM!BAM! Love it!

Delivered

   iMessage

Greg gone wild

June 15, 2017 at 2:05AM
Greg Smith greg@donots.com
To: Ben Rodgers rodgersconsulting12@gmail.com
Re: Genetics

One more picture. Me. Clearly in great shape. This is where Caleb should be at 16 if he follows my genetic map.

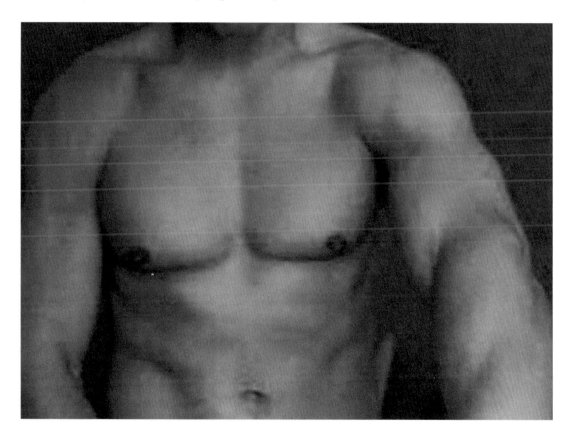

June 16, 2017 at 7:47
Greg Smith greg@donots.com
To: Ben Rodgers <u>rodgersconsulting12@gmail.com</u>
Re: EMAILS / PICTURE

Greg.

In my 15 years of coaching I cannot remember a parent ever sending me a picture of themselves with their shirt off. This needs to stop.

Ben

How's the other team look?

Seriously questioning birth dates. a couple of these girls are huge. size 12 feet

You know how that team rolls. They're probably college freshmen.

at least

wow! he's not starting the first line

That's weird

Delivered

it's really weird

now they're paying for it

painful

 iMessage

Score?

2-10

What! Why?

No D.

Is it that short kid?

They're all playing like shit

2-11

Jesus

Delivered

2-14

3-17

iMessage

The fuck is going on!

What is Lila doing? Anything?

not really. doesn't want the ball

Go over to the bench and say something to her

I'm not doing that

Do it!

Delivered

> iMessage

June 20, 2017 at 5:13 PM
Molly Green laxmommie@gmail.com
To: Team Moms bbc: Hank Rawlings

Re: Re; Surprise Coach gift 💔

Hi Moms,

The following families have not contributed to coach Rawlings gift:

Jason Simmons (midfield, #14, Man-up team)
Matt Daly (Defense #99 / also LSM)
Rodger Wright (Attack #2)
Duke Brown (#15 Goalie)
Ben McDaniels (#21 midfield)

If you decide you want to recognize all the hard work Coach Rawlings has put in helping our boys, please bring your check / cash to the game Saturday, after that it will be too late. The gift I am ordering for coach is handmade and takes time.

Molly
Evan (#13)

June 20, 2017 at 7:13 PM
Hank Rawlings hr200@us.gov
To: Molly Green laxmommie@gmail.com

Re: Re; Surprise Coach gift 💔

Hi Molly,

I really appreciate the thought but would prefer to be left off this thread.

H

June 20, 2017 at 7:23 PM
Molly Green laxmommie@gmail.com
To: Hank Rawlings hr200@us.gov

Re: Re; Surprise Coach gift 💝

Oops. Way over extended here coordinating the team cookout, washing jerseys, etc, etc! Did I get the kids numbers and positions right? I wasn't sure.

June 20, 2017 at 7:40 PM
Hank Rawlings hr200@us.gov
To: Molly Green laxmommie@gmail.com

Re; Re; Surprise Coach gift 💝

Yes.

June 20, 2017 at 7:55 PM
Molly Green   laxmommie@gmail.com
To: Hank Rawlings hr200@us.gov

Re: Re; Surprise Coach gift 💝

Ben McDaniels is a Middie? That's so puzzling to me. Seems like Attack would be better fit given his medical issues. That way he can just stand there and wait for someone to bring him the ball.

June 20, 2017 at 8:13 PM
Hank Rawlings hr200@us.gov
To: Molly Green laxmommie@gmail.com

Re: Re; Surprise Coach gift 💝

what medical issues?

June 20, 2017 at 8:20 PM
Molly Green   laxmommle@gmail.com
To: Hank Rawlings hr200@us.gov
Re: Re; Surprise Coach gift 💔

He seems slower then the rest of the kids. I took a video of him running if you want to see it.

June 20, 2017 at 9:25 PM
Hank Rawlings hr200@us.gov
To: Molly Green laxmommie@gmail.com
Re: Re; Surprise Coach gift 💔

There are no medical issues. It's my policy not to discuss other players with parents.

June 20, 2017 at 9:45 PM
Molly Green laxmommie@gmail.com
Hank Rawlings hr200@us.gov
Re: Re; Surprise Coach gift 💔

Ok. Would it be possible for you to send me a list of returning players / kids signed up for tryouts
so I can get a head count for next years squad.

June 21, 2017 at 8:30 AM
Hank Rawlings hr200@us.gov
To: Molly Green laxmommie@gmail.com
Re: Re; Surprise Coach gift 💔

I'm not clear why you would need that information and I'm not releasing the roster for tryouts. We always have 22
kids per team, no matter what.

June 21, 2017 at 8:45 AM
Molly Green laxmommie@gmail.com
To: Hank Rawlings hr200@us.gov
Re: Re; Surprise Coach gift 💔

Sounds good. And I'm glad Ben is ok. I was really worried about him.

June 21, 2017 at 10:00 PM
Phil Webb Phil@BigBank.net
To: Guadalupe Hernandez GHern@aol.com

Re: Jose

Hola padres de José nos gustaría tener a José a nuestra casa y adoptarlo. Somos libres todos los días de la semana. Déjame saber qué día funciona para ti. El amor poco mans hustle.

Phil Webb

Wendy

Do you think we should sign Lila up for the eastside clinic? Its after practice at 8? Everyone on the team is doing it.

Sure

Wendy

she'll have to eat dinner and do her homework in the car. do you think its too much?

Not sure about that. She has trouble seeing her homework in the car.

Wendy

She can use a head lamp.

OK. I think it's probably worth it then. She looks terrible the season.

Lila

Dad. I'm on this thread.

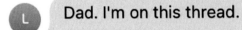 iMessage

June 22, 2017 at 2:23AM
Greg Smith greg@donots.com
To: Ben Rodgers rodgersconsulting12@gmail.com
Re: a little about me..

First of all. I want to apologize for my last email and the photo. I work very hard to stay in shape and sometimes my pride takes the wheel. That said, I feel like I have burdened you with too much information about Caleb and I want you to know that I am going to stop doing that. My intention was to give you a window into Caleb's world, that's it. Nobody was there for me as a kid and I know how much you care. It means a lot to me that Caleb has you to lean on. I was extremely over weight as a kid and a compulsive eater. I used food to replace the emotional void left by my father, who for whatever reason, rejected me. At about age 12 I found hockey and the pounds started to melt away. I also was a very good player. Around age 17 I was drafted by the Oilers. At that point I felt a lot of pressure to finally make my father proud. Believe it or not just getting drafted wasn't enough. Unfortunately due to the stress, I started drinking and then fell into compulsive sexual activity with strangers. After a bad week at the Oilers training camp that involved some poor choices in an Arby's restroom (don't worry, I wasn't there for the food) the Oilers cut me. Then I spent two months in Vegas gambling away everything I had. About that time my dad died. So as you can imagine, at that point I hated who I had become. I hitch-hiked back to Boston and took a job working on a road crew just outside of Revere. On that job I met a guy named Richie P. I credit this man with saving my life. He was fresh out of prison and basically had seen it all. Everyday we would sit and eat lunch. He usually brought soup which he shared with me (I couldn't afford lunch). He always brought two spoons. He would talk about prison and what he had to endure and he started to really build me up. He said he saw my potential. I told him about Arby's and all the meth stuff, and he literally didn't care. He and I decided to quit the road crew and open a pretzel cart down by the Boston Garden. We both had always loved soft pretzels and had some pretty cutting edge ideas related to toppings, etc. I was pretty good with chemicals and figured I could handle the baking. That was the beginning of DoughKnots. We made pretzels until our hands were raw. Soon enough I met my wife Jane. She was also making some life changes (had done some swinging, didn't love it) and we really got each other on a no bullshit level. But here I was 28, DoughKnots was taking off, I had this beautiful wife and new baby and the pressure was intense. What did I do? You guessed it. Right back into old habits. After I woke up by the side of the Charles River next to a Craigslist date who lied to me about her original plumbing (need I say more) I knew I had finally hit bottom. That was it; no more meth, no more stranger sex, definitely no more swinging. I moved the family to Weston and the wife and I kept a very low profile; dinners at home, antique roadshow, no porn. At that point I found out Richie P. had embezzled 50K from DoughKnots and never paid the IRS. As you might imagine the Feds were after us, so Jane and I drove all our valuables up to my uncle's house in Canada and then drove back and declared bankruptcy. The Feds took our house and our three cars. Thankfully, we managed to claw our way out of that hole and start a new pretzel business; DoNots. It's a take on DoughKnots. The name is also a helpful reminder for me each day; "Do not" screw up again. So I'm good now. Anyway, you've probably figured out the point of this email, in other words; are you in need of an assistant coach? I'd love to help out with the team. -G

July 1, 2017 at 6:47 PM
Jim Black jimandkaren@organics.org
To: Phil Webb Phil@BigBank.net
Re: adopting jose ???

Bill. Did you email the Hernandez family about adopting Jose?

Jim
"If you're going through hell, keep going." - Winston Churchill

July 1, 2017 at 7:01 PM
Phil Webb phil@BigBank.net
To: Jim Black jimandkaren@organics.org
Re: adopting jose ???

no I asked for a playdate.

sent from my iphone
all thumbs

July 1, 2017 at 7:05 PM
Jim Black jimandkaren@organics.org
To: Phil Webb phil@BigBank.net
Re: adopting jose ???

you didn't. you asked to adopt him. i've seen the email

Jim
"If you're going through hell, keep going." - Winston Churchill

July 1, 2017 at 7:19 PM
Phil **Webb** ph**il@BigBank.net**
To: Jim **Black** jimandkaren@organics.org
Re: adopting jose ???

I used Google translate.

sent from my iphone
all thumbs

July 1, 2017 at 9:02 PM
Jim Black jimandkaren@organics.org
To Phil **Webb** ph**il@BigBank.net**
Re: adopting jose ???

it didn't work correctly. the family is very upset. we're in unchartered territory here bill. i need to ask you to stop contacting the family or speaking to their son. if you can't do that I will have to remove lucas from the team.

Jim
"If you're going through hell, keep going." - *Winston Churchill*

July 5, 2017 at 9:12 PM
Jeff Sullivan SullyMA@aol.com
To: Ben Rodgers rodgersconsulting12@gmail.com **David Brown; Jeff Sullivan** SullyMA@aol.com;
David Brown brownfamily_1975@earthlink.net
Re: My turn

Wow. This was tucked in my car door after practice. -Sully

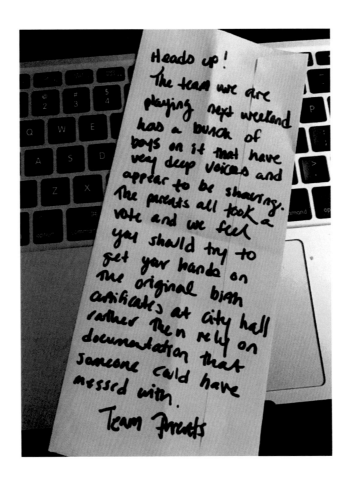

July 5, 2017 at 9:45 PM
Ben Rodgers <u>rodgersconsulting12@gmail.com</u>
To: Jeff Sullivan <u>SullyMA@aol.com</u>
Re: My turn

Why don't you go down to city hall and pull the birth certificates of the entire team roster? that seems reasonable. Ha Ha! B

July 7, 2017 at 7:05 PM
Phil Webb phil@BigBank.net
To: Jim Black jimandkaren@organics.org bcc: BGTSlaw.org
Re: lawsuit

Jim. I have contacted an attorney. Lucas will be at practice tomorrow at 5 sharp. You have no legal grounds by which you can remove him from the team. I think you know that.

sent from my iphone
all thumbs

July 8, 2017 at 9 AM
Jim Black jimandkaren@organics.org
To: Phil Webb phil@BigBank.net bbc: stienwaylawgroup.com
Re: Re: lawsuit

Phil.

I don't believe that I said I was removing Lucas, but rather _would_ remove him from the team if you could not stop harassing Jose and his family. The Mini Mighties is a private club. I have the authority to remove your son from the team at any time.

Jim
"Respect was invented to cover the empty place where love should be."
— *Leo Tolstoy*

July 16, 2017 at 1:30 AM
Greg Smith greg@donots.com
To: Ben Rodgers <u>rodgersconsulting12@gmail.com</u>
Re: a little poem I wrote

Hi There stranger! You've been radio silent. I hope everything is okay on your end! I'd love your feedback on this poem. I think it really works and might be something the team would respond to for inspiration, etc. Happy to make copies and distribute before the big game Friday.

<u>The Athlete</u>

It's 5am.
Should I run, lift or bike?
Days like this I should probably hike.
To the top of a mountain or somewhere grand.
But instead I will just stand.
Stand here and think about who I could've been.
All the things I wanted to win.
The moments of grim poor decision sin. **(this line is really strong I think!**)
That stole the promise of a guy with potential.
Who now most days doesn't make enough to cover his dental.
But that's okay because I will never quit
Never quit fighting till the buzzer sounds
And I turn to the team and I am hoisted high in the air
The hero who never quit.

I know the last two lines are missing something so feel free to jump in there and add what inspires you! Team work baby! -GDog

L Don't get mad Mom and Dad.

Wendy

W what is it???

Lila

L I quit.

Wendy

W you quit what?

> iMessage

Lila

Basketball

 iMessage

July 29, 2017 at 3:13 AM
Greg Smith greg@donots.com
To: Ben Rodgers rodgersconsulting12@gmail.com
Re: WTF

Coach.

I haven't heard back from you about the poem or some of the personal information I shared. Just so you know, **NOBODY**, and I mean **NO ONE**, other than my wife and my parole officer know about that stuff. It was very hard for me to share that with you and I have to say I am **REALLY** disappointed you haven't responded to me. Today at practice I felt like you were avoiding me and deliberately moving to the other side of the rink. You **OWE** me a response. We pay 15K a year to watch our son sit on that bench and the least you can do is take the fucking time to get back to me.

My cell is 617-555-1694

Greg

July 29, 2017 at 3: 45 AM
Greg Smith greg@donuts.com
To: Ben Rodgers <u>rodgersconsulting12@gmail.com</u>
Re: WTF

I'm sorry. That last email was stronger then I intended. I don't do well with abandonment. It pushes every button on my keyboard. My dad did the best he could with what he had. I just keep telling myself that. He did his best.
Greg

July 29, 2017 at 4: 20 AM
Greg Smith greg@donuts.com
To: Ben Rodgers <u>rodgersconsutling12@gmail.com</u>
Re: WTF

I can't stop crying. I think my dad loved me.

July 30, 2017 at 7:45 AM
Ben Rodgers rodgersconsulting12@gmail.com
To: Boys 5/6 Elite Coaches
Re: problem parent

Hi Coaches

Today I woke up to a string of emails from Greg Smith (Caleb's father). There was a man in a car sitting outside my house this morning. The guy was wearing a hat and sunglasses but I'm pretty sure it was Greg Smith. I've instituted my "crazy parent protocol" on this one and just ignored most of the emails, but at this point I think we actually have a problem. He is not letting up.

See attached emails. I'd love some guidance here.

July 30, 2017 at 8:01
David Brown brownfamily_1975@earthlink.net
To: Ben Rodgers rodgersconsulting12@gmail.com
Re: Re: problem parent

Are you freaking kidding me! The selfie in the mirror is a deal breaker for me. The kid is off the team. Period. -DB

July 30, 2017 at 8:03
Tom McDonald tom_kath6@gmail.com
To: Ben Rodgers rodgersconsulting12@gmail.com
Re: Re: problem parent

I agree with David. Unfortunate for the kid. Nice kid.
Tom

July 30, 2017 at 8:15
Jeff Sullivan <u>SullyMA@aol.com</u>
To: <u>rodgersconsulting12@gmail.com</u>
Re: Re: problem parent

Why don't you just put dad on the team Ben. Ha ha! - Sully.

Suck up lax mom

Hank Rawlings **hr200@us.gov**
To: Team Parents
Re: my coaches gift

Aug 4, 2017 at 7:09

Thanks everyone for the oil painting. I don't own a horse, but I imagine it would be fun to ride one and it's nice having a picture of me on one. Some of you had requested a pix of the painting. Here's a photo

Aug 5, 2017 at 3:45 PM
Molly Green laxmommie@gmail.com
Hank Rawlings hr200@us.gov
Re: my coaches gift

Hank. I am really furious. Linda McDaniels (Ben #21 short, no left, no cradle, slow, no shot midfielder) told me you were an avid horse back rider and horse art collector. I have no idea why she would say something like that when it wasn't true. I think she is trying to cast me in a bad light before tryouts. The boys are both competing for playing time and at this point I think she is simply desperate to get Ben on the field. Messing with me was a huge mistake. Messing with my kid was her last mistake. Trust me. I am furious!

Molly

Sept 1, 2017 at 8:19 PM
Hank Rawlings hr200@us.gov
Molly Green laxmommie@gmail.com
Re: Team roster

Dear Molly,

We enjoyed coaching Evan this summer. As you know tryouts were extremely competitive. Unfortunately at this point we are unable to offer Evan a spot on the Fall team. These decisions are never easy ones for us. We hope he will tryout next season.

Hank

Sept 27, 2017 at 3:45 PM
Molly Green laxmommie@gmail.com
Hank Rawlings hr200@us.gov
Re: Damages

Mr Rawlings,

Please see attached invoice for damages related to our exposure to your program.

GREEN FAMILY INVOICE FOR WASTED MONEY AND TIME WHILE YOU PRETENDED TO GIVE A SHIT ABOUT OUR SONS FUTURE ON YOUR FUCKING TEAM!

Description	Quantity	Unit Price	Cost
Sitting on the bench for no reason	5 hours	$ 150	$ 750
Hotel nights traveling for a team that didn't play him	8	$ 120	$ 960
Gear we bought thinking he was getting back on team	1	$ 450	$ 450
Therapy to cope with his disapointment	3 hours	$ 200	$ 600
Therapy to cope with my disapointment	7 hours	$ 300	$ 2,100
		Subtotal	$ 4,860
	Tax	8.25%	$ 401
		Total	$ 5,261

Please refund our money in the next ten business days.

Guadalupe Hernandez GHern@aol.com
To: Phil Webb phil@BigBank.net

Estimado Sr. Webb

Lo más importante que aprendemos de los deportes no tiene nada que ver con ganar o perder. Los atletas reales pueden decirle que así como la mayoría de los niños de kindergarten. Rezaré por tí.

Guadalupe

Translation: "The most important thing we learn from sports has nothing to do with winning or losing. Real athletes can tell you this as well as most kindergarten children. I will pray for you."

i'm feeling badly about lila and basketball

I know. me too

should we see if she wants to try out for another team?

I don't think the team is issue.

what are you saying?

Are you saying it's me?

It was probably

I just wanted her to have fun. was it me?

It was probably

Me too

Delivered

 iMessage

Burned out Ted

Ted Nichols TdN@hotmail.com
To: Charles Hentz chuck.TriHigh.org   Sept 13, 2017 at 6:00 PM
Re: Thanks

Dear Chuck,

Coaching the girls varsity soccer team at Trident High School has been the highlight of my adult life. As you know all three of my girls played for Trident. Every spring the smell of freshly cut grass conjures up memories of decades of doing what I love. I am really going to miss it. The decision was not an easy one.

Carol and I are going to spend next soccer season relaxing, traveling and taking some cooking classes. I understand David Hillman is being considered as my replacement. I'm sure he'll do fine. He's pretty dedicated.

Thanks so very much,

Coach Ted.

Made in the USA
Columbia, SC
26 July 2017